PLATE TECTONICS
and Disasters

By Tom Greve

Rourke
Educational Media
rourkeeducationalmedia.com

www.rourkeeducationalmedia.com

PHOTO CREDITS:
Front Cover: © Michael Utech; Table of contents © Wojciech Jarosz; Page 4-5 © youding xie; Page 6 © Victor Zastol`skiy; Page 7 © The Power of Forever Photography, Linda Bair; Page 8 © Pzaxe; Page 10 © Baris Simsek; Page 11 © Tilmann von Au; Page 12 © Tomi Tenetz; Page 13 © Michal Bryc, Frank Ramspott, Craig Stocks; Page 14 © montiannoowong, Frenta; Page 15 © grimgram; Page 16 © Mopic, visdia; Page 17 © Ammit, Shutterbas, Stephan Hoerold, Justin Reznick, Josef Friedhuber; Page 18 © yoshiyayo; Page 19 © chuong vu; Page 21 © Creativeye99, Princeton University Archives; Page 22 © Michelle Gibson, Arsgera; Page 23 © Jonathan Barton, Petr Podrouzek; Page 24 © Daulon; Page 25 © Spirinaelena, Jan Rysavy; Page 26 © Andreus, Steven Prorak; Page 27 © crossroadscreative, Josef Friedhuber , Vampy1; Page 28 © John_ Woodcock, Claudia Dewald; Page 29 © Robert Paul Van Beets, NASA; Page 30 © Floriano Rescigno, Martin Lladó; Page 31 © Nataliya Hora, jamesbenet; Page 32 © Rudvi; Page 33 © National Archives and Records Administration, Library of Congress; Page 35 © Jeremy Mayes, Wisconsinart; Page 36 © U.S. federal government, Banol2007; Page 37 © Hunor Focze; Page 38 © United States Geological Survey; Page 39 © U.S. National Oceanic and Atmospheric Administration, Arindam Banerjee; Page 40 © U.S. National Oceanic and Atmospheric Administration, kickers; Page 41 © United States Government, University of California; Page 42 © Ron and Patty Thomas Photography; Page 43 © U.S. Department of the Interior, Creative Commons, Johanfo at en.wikipedia; Page 44-45 © Dusan Todorovic;

Edited by Precious McKenzie

Cover design & interior layout by Cory Davis

Library of Congress PCN Data

Plate Tectonics and Disasters / Tom Greve
(Let's Explore Science)
ISBN 978-1-61810-122-8 (hard cover - English) (alk. paper)
ISBN 978-1-61810-255-3 (soft cover - English)
ISBN 978-1-61810-382-6 (e-Book - English)
ISBN 978-1-63155-088-1 (hard cover - Spanish) (alk. paper)
ISBN 978-1-62717-312-4 (soft cover - Spanish)
ISBN 978-1-62717-513-5 (e-Book - Spanish)
Library of Congress Control Number: 2011945266

Also Available as:
ROURKE'S e-Books

Rourke Educational Media
Printed in the United States of America,
North Mankato, Minnesota

rourkeeducationalmedia.com
customerservice@rourkeeducationalmedia.com • PO Box 643328 Vero Beach, Florida 32964

PLATE TECTONICS
and Disasters

Meg Greve

Table of Contents

CHAPTER ONE

UNDERSTANDING WHAT WE'RE STANDING OVER

What is the nature of the ground beneath our feet? In many ways, the answer depends on where a person is standing. The ground can be hard and rocky. It might be covered by soft grasses. In urban areas it may be covered by concrete. But most people take the ground for granted. We assume it is solidly underfoot, supporting us, our houses, and our cities.

Solid ground should not always be taken for granted. It is capable of moving, or changing shape. These movements are usually very slow and cannot even be detected. Other times, as in the case of an **earthquake**, the movement is sudden, violent, and catastrophic.

Earthquakes are dangerous, destructive, and sometimes deadly. They are the result of powerful forces working inside the Earth that can cause the ground to move, shake, or even break apart.

Humans have pondered the mysteries of Earth's ground movements since the dawn of recorded history. After all, earthquakes have been rumbling and volcanoes have been erupting for longer than humans have been around to witness them. So what makes the ground move or shake? What makes a mountain explode with fiery fury?

Scientific understanding and theories concerning the forces that cause volcanic eruptions and earthquakes have grown immensely in the past 100 years.

Geology and **paleontology**, or the scientific study of the Earth's rocks and the fossil remains of plants and animals, have helped other scientists form theories about the nature of the ground and its movements. The prevailing scientific theory of what makes the ground, the continents, even the floor of the ocean move or change shape, is known as the theory of plate tectonics.

Fossil dig sites like Fossil Butte National Monument have helped scientists piece together theories on how similar fossils have been found in different continents and climates. This can be seen as evidence of continental movement over time.

PLATE PERSPECTIVE:

Plate tectonics refers to geological plates, or large rigid slabs of rock. Tectonics comes from the Greek word meaning "to build". The term plate tectonics refers to the scientific study of how the Earth's outer surface is constantly being built and rebuilt by a series of slowly moving plates.

As a scientific theory, plate tectonics is built upon previous theories proven to be scientific facts. Scientists then test new theories in an ongoing effort to advance collective scientific knowledge.

Until early in the 20th century, much of the study of Earth's physical surface assumed the planet's continents were **stationary**. But one feature of Earth's modern continental map made some scientists revisit this theory.

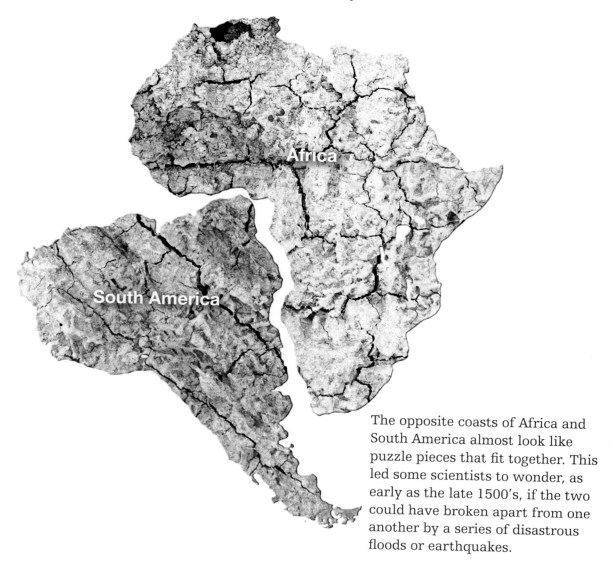

The opposite coasts of Africa and South America almost look like puzzle pieces that fit together. This led some scientists to wonder, as early as the late 1500's, if the two could have broken apart from one another by a series of disastrous floods or earthquakes.

PLATE TECTONIC PIONEER

In 1912, German scientist Alfred Wegener put forth the theory of continental drift. His theory was based on fossil evidence that showed the existence of the same plants and animals on separate continents in differing climates. Since they could not have crossed the ocean as living organisms, Wegener reasoned the continents had once been joined. He theorized that over millions of years the continents had drifted to their current locations.

Wegener could not identify the forces causing the movement, and his theory was largely ignored during his lifetime. After his death, the theory of continental drift would spark the scientific discoveries leading to the current understanding of plate tectonics.

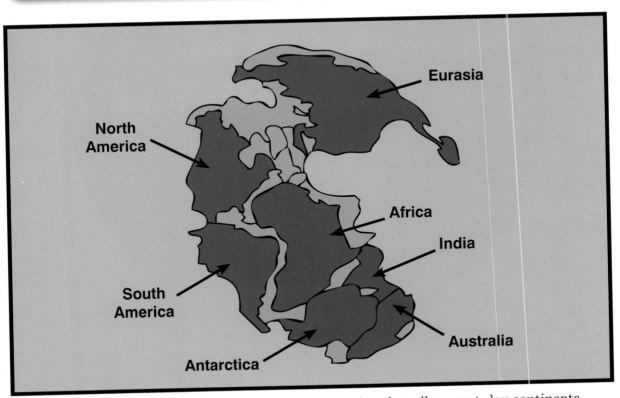

Wegener's continental drift theory included his assertion that all present-day continents were once a single land mass he called Pangea, meaning "all Earth."

The theory of plate tectonics provides a scientific explanation for the movement of the Earth's crust from the gradual shift to the **cataclysmic** break. It also explains the spectacular role of volcanoes. It is a theory based on proven scientific ideas about the physical makeup of the Earth's interior and the **dynamic** nature of its crust, including the continents, mountain ranges, and ocean floors.

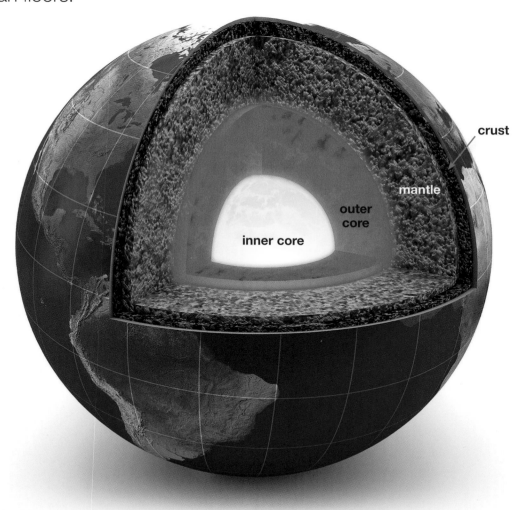

crust

mantle

outer core

inner core

Deep inside Earth, there is a magnetized core made of heavy metal. Around the inner core there is an outer core of super-heated liquid metal. Further from the center, Earth has a thick layer of rock called the mantle. Surrounding the mantle is Earth's outermost layer of rock called the crust. The top of the crust is the planet's actual surface, known as the ground on which we walk.

Plate tectonics is based on the idea that forces deep inside Earth can cause the massive plates making up the Earth's crust to move, expand, collide, and overlap. The greatest of these forces are immense heat and pressure. Super-heated, pressurized rock can rise or flow through sections of Earth's. Eventually, this heated rock might emerge onto the surface.

The plates making up the Earth's crust move atop the planet's super-heated liquid interior. Sometimes, currents of melted rock from deep inside the Earth emerge onto the planet's surface in the form of an erupting volcano.

CHAPTER TWO

FROM CORE TO CRUST: FINDING FAULT IN THE EARTH'S PLATES

Earth's crust serves as the planet's top layer of skin. Compared to the planet's core and mantle, it is shallow and brittle, like the cracked shell of a hard boiled egg.

Structures must be built to withstand the forces that move the Earth.

The lines along which two plates come together are known as plate boundaries. Most of Earth's plate boundaries are located under the ocean. The few that exist on dry land have proven valuable to scientific study. Scientists monitor the depth and power of those movements. This is the science of **seismology**. Seismologists see Earth's surface as plates divided by plate boundaries rather than as continents divided by oceans.

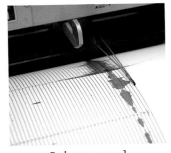

Seismograph

San Andreas Fault

Earth's most notorious plate boundary is California's San Andreas Fault. It runs along a section between the Pacific plate and the North American plate. Seismologists from the United States Geological Survey (U.S.G.S.) constantly monitor the fault line for seismic activity.

The thickness of crust plates vary. They are between 15 and 40 miles (25 and 65 kilometers) thick along the dry land of the continents, but only about 5 miles (8 kilometers) thick underneath the oceans.

If a slice of the planet's interior could be extracted, it would show the multiple layers from core to crust.

Because Earth's crust is thinner under the ocean, and since oceans cover more than 70 percent of Earth's surface, most of the planet's active seismic locations are underneath the ocean.

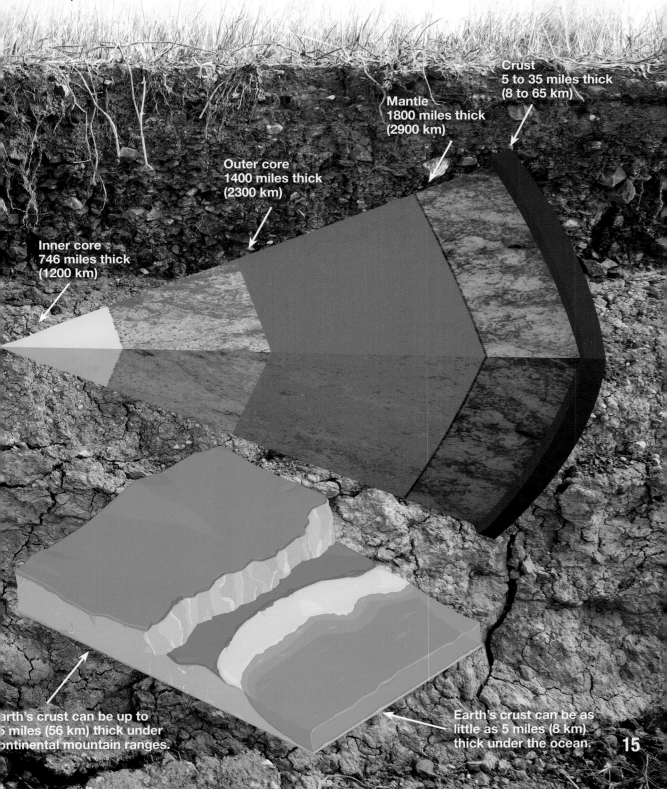

Crust
5 to 35 miles thick
(8 to 65 km)

Mantle
1800 miles thick
(2900 km)

Outer core
1400 miles thick
(2300 km)

Inner core
746 miles thick
(1200 km)

arth's crust can be up to
miles (56 km) thick under
ontinental mountain ranges.

Earth's crust can be as
little as 5 miles (8 km)
thick under the ocean.

15

Earth's core is very, very hot. It is nearly as hot as the Sun. Because it is thousands of miles underground, scientists can only theorize an approximate temperature at Earth's core of about 9,000 to 13,000 degrees Fahrenheit (5,000 and 7,000 degrees Celsius). Incredible compression prevents the metal inner core from melting. The outer core, on the other hand, is percolating with immensely hot, liquid metal. The heat flows outward into the mantle and toward the planet's surface. In the same way that warm air rises toward the ceiling of a room and cold air drops toward the floor, **convection** currents cause the intense heat to rise through the mantle.

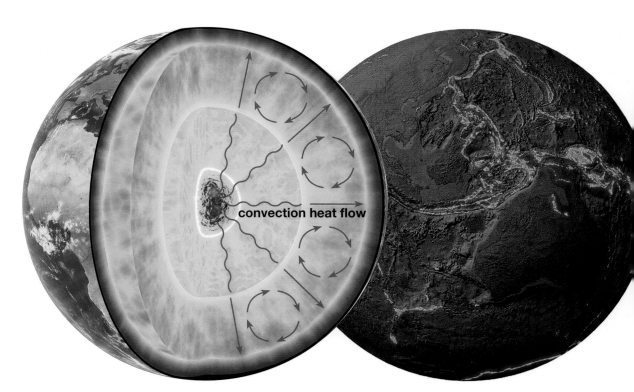

convection heat flow

Constant convection heat currents push liquefied mantle rock outward into the underside of the crust where massive pressure builds up.

As the heat rises, its intensity causes parts of the rock in the mantle to flow ever closer to the crust as cooler, solid rock descends. This flowing rock is called magma. Since the thinnest part of Earth's crust is under the oceans, rising magma can usually get closer to the Earth's surface under water than it can on dry land. Once the magma finds a way through Earth's crust, it becomes like incredibly hot toothpaste flowing out of a squeezed tube. Magma that rises onto Earth's surface is called lava.

Few spots on Earth provide as clear an indicator of fearsome tectonic forces in action as Mount Kilauea in Hawaii. The volcano has been spewing liquid rock from inside the Earth continuously since 1983.

The forces of intense geologic heat and pressure over millions of years can create mountain ranges or islands. They can also unleash seismic violence onto the Earth's surface, causing human tragedies like earthquakes and **tsunamis**.

Japan

Powerful seismic activity under the ocean can set off a massive displacement of water. This is called a tsunami. An earthquake beneath the Pacific Ocean in March of 2011 sent a massive tsunami into Japan's east coast, causing immense devastation and death.

Great East Japan Earthquake, March 2011

CHAPTER THREE
MAJESTIES: OCEANS DEEP, MOUNTAINS HIGH

The **expulsion** of magma through volcanic plate boundaries in the seafloor pushes Earth's crustal plates up, into what's called a mid-oceanic ridge. It also pushes the two plates apart. Geologists call this action seafloor spreading.

SEISMIC SAMPLER

There are three primary types of tectonic plate boundaries.

Divergent boundaries are where two plates move apart. This is what happens during seafloor spreading.

Convergent boundaries are when two plates collide or push into one another.

Transform boundaries are when two plates slide past each other along their common edge.

Seafloor spreading causes two plates to move apart along the plate boundary at the bottom of the ocean. As magma releases through the **rift**, it cools and becomes part of the rocky plate moving slowly away from the boundary. A divergence along one boundary causes plates to converge, or **transform**, along different boundaries with other neighboring plates in a sort of plate tectonic chain reaction collision.

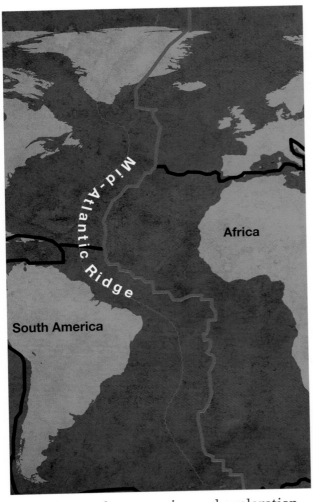

Thanks to modern mapping and exploration, scientists have definitive evidence of a massive mountain ridge plate boundary running along the bottom of the Atlantic Ocean. This divergent boundary is called the Mid-Atlantic Ridge, and it's very slowly pushing the African and South American plates further apart.

PLATE TECTONIC PIONEER:

Harry Hess was a geology professor and Navy officer who captained a U.S. ship during World War II. During the war, he used sonar instruments on his ship to map the floor of the Pacific Ocean. In 1960, his theory of seafloor spreading held that molten rock emissions through underwater plate boundaries had not only caused a mountainous ridge to form along the ocean floor, but was causing Earth's plates along the ridge to spread apart. This idea is considered the key scientific link between Wegener's original theory of continental drift and the modern scientific study of plate tectonics.

Collisions between Earth's converging crustal plates are gradual. But over time, the pressure from one plate running into another can literally create, and move, mountains. Many of the mountain ranges on Earth's continents are the result of plate buckling, or crumpling, under **convergent** pressure.

The average upward thrust speed of a buckling crust plate is very slow. Some geologists describe mountain formation happening at a similar rate as human fingernail growth.

Imagine laying two small rugs on a wood floor. If the rugs are gently pushed against each other, the less rigid of the two rugs will begin to crumple. If both rugs are too rigid to crumple, the edge of one rug may push up and over the other until they either overlap or come to rest standing upright against each other. This is the nature of convergent plate tectonics, except what might take 10 seconds to illustrate with two rugs takes millions of years to happen with two of Earth's crustal plates.

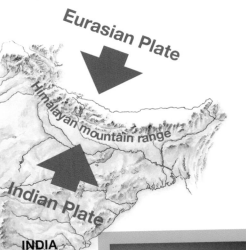

Like an enormous crumpled rug, the Himalayan mountain range in Asia is an example of convergent plate tectonic forces. It is the result of the Indian plate pushing into the Eurasian plate, causing it to buckle, or crumple upward.

Like one stiff rug sliding under another as they get pushed together, convergent collisions of crustal plates can result in one plate overlapping the other. This motion is known as **subduction**. Unlike the rugs on a hardwood floor, Earth's crustal plates can get pushed back down into the mantle.

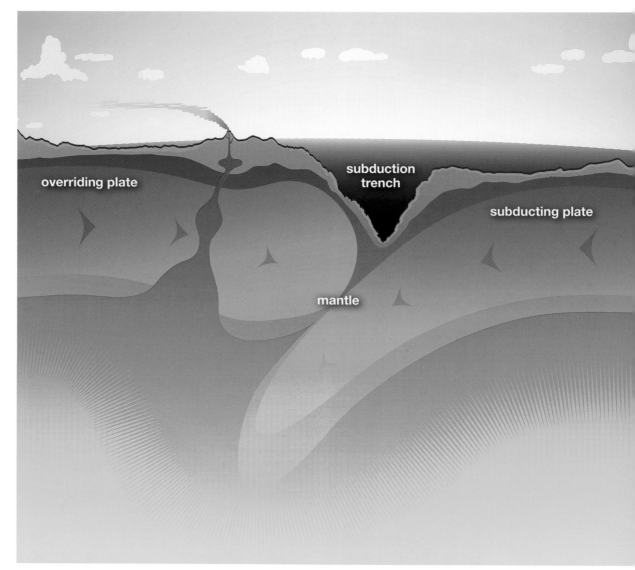

As the leading edge of a subducting plate descends into Earth's mantle, magma often rises through the overriding plate, forming volcanoes at the surface.

The front edge of the plate being subducted gets pushed downward into Earth's hot mantle by the overriding plate. The front edge of the overriding plate can get caught and deformed, or bent downward, by the movement of the subducting plate. This action creates oceanic trenches.

Forbidden Island Saipan, North Marianas

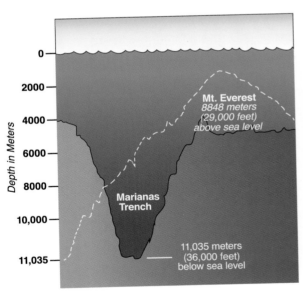

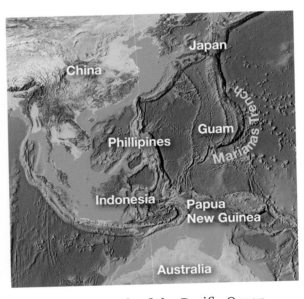

The deepest known spot on Earth's crust is the Marianas Trench of the Pacific Ocean. The trench is created by the Pacific plate subducting under the leading edge of the much smaller Mariana plate. The seafloor at the trenches deepest point is more than 36,000 feet (11,000 meters) beneath the ocean's surface. It is so deep that if you took Mount Everest, Earth's tallest mountain, from the Himalayas and set it in the trench, the tip of the mountain would still be 7,166 feet (2,183 meters) under water.

The plate tectonic process of subduction also triggers what geologists call volcanism, or the creation of volcanoes. When the leading edge of a subducting plate descends back into the hot mantle, the pressurized and intensely hot interaction causes magma to begin its convection flow back toward the crust. Volcanoes provide passageways for magma expulsion and pressure release along Earth's crust.

Though its exact origins remain a mystery, Devil's Tower in Wyoming offers evidence of an ancient magma flow that cooled as rock and sediment around it eroded.

volcano

magma

Devil's Tower, Wyoming

Sometimes the pressure of magma pushing through Earth's crust doesn't necessarily happen along plate boundaries but instead pushes up through the center of an oceanic plate. These are called geologic hot spots. As expelled lava cools under the water, it begins to accumulate into a large mound with more lava flowing out of the top. This process continues until a massive underwater mountain forms. Over millions of years, as magma continues to flow up from Earth's mantle, that volcanic mountain can grow until its top is above the ocean's surface, creating an island. This is how the Hawaiian islands were likely formed.

Kaui Oahu Maui
Hawaii

PACIFIC PLATE

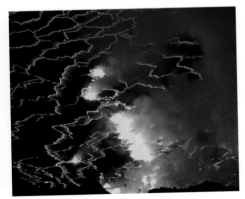

Most of Earth's divergent plate boundaries are under water. But two spots offer rare glimpses into the volcanic activity of a divergent boundary on land. In November of 2011, the Nyamuragira volcano erupted with spectacular force.

Iceland's Grimsvotn Volcanic eruption from March 2010

Iceland is being slowly split in two. That's because it sits directly on the Mid-Atlantic Ridge plate boundary.

While both **divergent** and convergent tectonic plate boundaries involve volcanic activity, transform boundaries usually do not. Plate movement along transform boundaries involves one plate sliding alongside another.

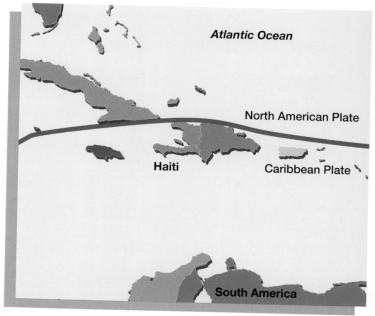

The January 2010 earthquake, which decimated the island nation of Haiti, happened along the transform boundary between the Caribbean plate and the North American plate.

Despite the absence of pressurized magma from Earth's mantle, transform boundary movements are capable of more devastating seismic **catastrophes**. Plate tectonic movements, whether divergent, convergent, or transform, are often deadly events of historic proportions.

GLOBAL GIVE AND TAKE

Earth's size is constant. It does not grow or shrink because of expanding divergent or subducting plates. This is known as the zero-sum game of plate tectonics. The divergent action of seafloor spreading in one part of Earth's crust is generally equal to the convergent action of subduction, or transformation, somewhere else.

CHAPTER FOUR

TRAGEDIES: EARTHQUAKES AND THE RING OF FIRE

The **astronomical** force of plate tectonic action is capable of overwhelming all life on the planet. Living near a plate boundary or volcano means living with the possibility of catastrophic ground movements. The ground buckles, buildings fall apart, and mountains explode with violence. The geologic forces at work inside the Earth can create chaos and death on the planet's surface. It's a reality that has affected humankind throughout recorded history.

Among the most violent tectonic disasters happened in 79 AD. Italy's Mount Vesuvius erupted, covering the city of Pompeii with lava and burning ash. The force of the eruption was so sudden many victims were buried alive.

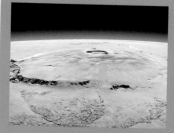

MAGMA ON MARS?

The plate tectonic forces happening inside the Earth that create volcanoes may be at work inside other planets as well. Satellite images of the planet Mars show the presence of a massive mountain far taller than any found on Earth. The mountain, which scientists call Olympus Mons, appears to have Calderas, or collapsed domes of cooled magma. Scientists think this is evidence of volcanic activity on Mars.

Earthquakes and volcanic eruptions are the result of released plate tectonic pressure that gets seen or felt on the Earth's surface.

Most earthquakes happen when a moving plate, caught or snagged on another plate along a convergent or transform boundary. Then it breaks free and jerks back to its original movement position. The point on the ground above where the plates break free from one another is called the quake's epicenter.

SEISMIC SCOREKEEPING: THE RICHTER MAGNITUDE SCALE

Seismograph

Seismologists use a complicated mathematical device called the Richter scale to determine relative intensity or magnitude of earthquakes. First developed in 1935 by California Technology Institute professor Charles Richter, it used seismograph readings to determine the energy released by a single seismic event. The scale does not judge an earthquake by how much damage it causes, merely the energy it releases.

The scale is a times-ten logarithm, meaning a 5.0 earthquake is actually ten times more powerful than a 4.0. The scale starts at 0.0 but has no top end. The most powerful earthquakes on record have topped 9.0 on the scale.

Transform boundaries like the San Andreas Fault are like two jagged edged chunks of concrete grinding along each other's surface. When irregular surfaces on the plate edges snag, their gradual progression slows and as their snagging points grind into one another, immense pressure builds. When the moving plate breaks free, all that built-up pressure releases suddenly, causing the moving plate, and the ground, to jump, often with destructive consequences.

The occasional release of energy from the plates sticking or snagging has rocked the city of San Francisco and surrounding areas many times, most notably in 1906 when a quake caused more than 3,000 deaths.

One fire hydrant remained active in San Francisco following the earthquake in 1906. Each year it is painted gold as a reminder of the role it played in saving the city.

SAN FRANCISCO'S TRANSFORM TRAGEDY

The massive 1906 quake along the San Andreas Fault was only the first part of what would become one of the worst disasters in U.S. history. Its severity toppled buildings and ruptured the city's gas and water lines. The gas ignited dozens of fires which quickly consumed much of the city over the course of four days and nights. Fire killed more people and destroyed more buildings than the actual earthquake. The quake of April 18, 1906 shed ominous light on the then-unknown forces at work along the San Andreas Fault.

Earthquakes along convergent plate boundaries involve different physical plate movements. The gradual rise of a mountain range due to the collision between converging plates can involve many earthquakes over time as the less dense of the two plates crumples up near the boundary.

Subduction, trench creation, and plate release recoil of a mega thrust quake.

One plate subducting under another underneath the ocean and above the mantle.

Subduction creates trench and deforms overriding plate.

Overriding plate breaks free and snaps back to former shape creating tsunami or megathrust earthquake.

Convergent plate subduction can result in the most powerful earthquakes. Known as **megathrust**

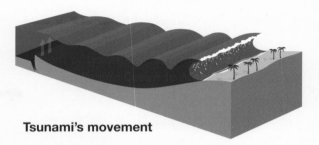

Tsunami's movement

earthquakes, they occur along subduction trenches on the ocean floor. In a megathrust earthquake, the overriding plate breaks free of the plate subducting beneath it and snaps back to its original position. This sudden thrust of the ocean's floor sends a massive amount of water toward the ocean's surface creating a tsunami.

The March 2011 earthquake and tsunami in Japan killed an estimated 15,700 people and left well over 100,000 homeless. It has raised questions about the placement and engineering of nuclear facilities near plate boundaries and coastlines.

Over the past century, all six of Earth's most powerful seismic events have been megathrust earthquakes. The most recent of these events devastated the east coast of Japan with a 9.0 magnitude earthquake in March of 2011. Not only did it destroy buildings and level entire neighborhoods, but it produced a tsunami that sent a giant wall of water rolling ashore from the Pacific Ocean. The force of the water washed away cars, boats, buildings, and people by the thousands. The quake badly damaged a nuclear power plant, leaving behind a deadly environmental hazard as well.

Despite the tragedies in Japan and California being separated by more than 5,000 miles (8,000 km) of ocean, they are both part of what geologists call the ring of fire. The ring refers to a 25,000 mile (40,000 km) long arc of plate boundaries almost entirely underneath the Pacific Ocean.

The ring of fire get its name because of its distinction as the source of nearly 90 percent of the seismic activity on Earth.

Three quarters of Earth's active volcanoes exist along the ring of fire. One of these, Washington state's Mount St. Helens, sits atop a subduction zone where the relatively small oceanic Juan de Fuca plate is subducting under the larger North American plate. It is the site of the most infamous volcanic eruption in American history.

Mount St. Helens

On the morning of May 18, 1980, the mountain's northern flank literally slid away in what geologists believe to be the largest landslide in recorded history. The landslide released a series of massive volcanic eruptions which blew the top 1300 feet (396 meters) clear off the mountain. The blast killed every living thing in a 230 square mile (595 square kilometer) area. Among the dead were 57 people, 21 of whom were never found.

Perhaps no two seismic events in the past century illustrate the overwhelming power of plate tectonic force more than the megathrust earthquake which struck Chile in 1960 and the transform boundary quake which hit Haiti in 2010.

The 9.5 magnitude Chile quake emanated from a subduction zone under the Pacific coast near the small town of Valdivia. An estimated 1600 people were killed in Chile, but the quake's power sent a tsunami wave clear across the Pacific Ocean strong enough to kill hundreds more in Hawaii, the Philippines, and Japan.

Haiti's 7.0 magnitude quake, though far less powerful than Chile's, was far more deadly. It was centered near the large, densely populated city of Port-Au-Prince. According to government estimates, more than 300,000 people died and more than a million were left homeless by the quake.

CHAPTER FIVE

PEOPLE AND PLATE TECTONICS

As much as science has helped humankind understand the nature of the forces at work beneath the ground, the timing and ferocity of Earth's seismic violence remains a mystery.

Earthquake prediction is difficult. Imprecise forecasts of possible seismic activity are called hazard assessments. They are based on an area's previous seismic events, which may only be known over the past several decades. In terms of geologic time, it's like trying to predict the outcome of a football game based on just one or two plays.

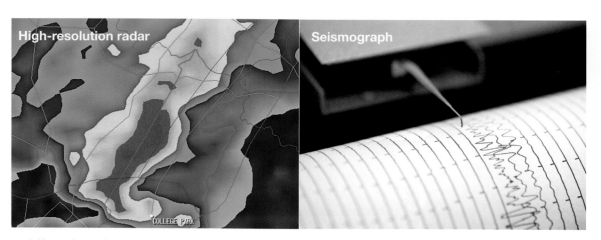

While a thunderstorm's arrival can be pinpointed by location and time, an earthquake, based on current technology and scientific understanding, cannot.

Reducing the loss of lives in the event of an earthquake may have more to do with structural engineering than actual forecasting.

Shake-table testing allows researchers to determine designs and construction practices that can withstand earthquakes. This research is especially crucial in large cities with tall buildings.

TESTING FOR TREMORS:
The University of California at Berkeley is home to the Pacific Earthquake Engineering Research Center. It is at the forefront of engineering earthquake-resistant structures.

As general geological understanding of plate movements has increased, so too has the specialized architectural engineering that can allow buildings and cities to better withstand earthquakes. Now many of San Francisco's older structures have undergone seismic **retrofitting** with braces or expandable parts to accommodate ground movement.

Bridges and tunnels, along with elevated roads and train tracks can be vulnerable to earthquakes. The San Francisco-Oakland Bay Bridge continues to undergo seismic retrofitting to keep it stable in the event of another quake.

Structures in the San Francisco area must meet strict engineering guidelines before they can be built. These guidelines are in place in other earthquake prone cities as well. They help ensure the buildings can withstand the effects of an earthquake without collapsing.

In 1989 one motorist was killed when a 6.9 magnitude quake struck San Francisco causing a section of the Oakland Bay bridge and a nearby elevated freeway to collapse. The quake also delayed the baseball World Series between the San Francisco Giants and the Oakland A's.

With no clear model for predicting specific seismic activity, and with Earth's populations expanding, humans will continue to live with the threats posed by tectonic plate movement and volcanic threats from deep underground.

After all, beneath the ground we stand on lies immense heat, pressure, and potentially deadly power. Earth remains a dynamic host to geological forces that even modern science hasn't yet fully understood. Those same forces, which drive the theory of plate tectonics, are modern yet ancient, slow yet explosive, mysterious yet unfolding in plain sight.

Scientists continue to study the awesome physical power, constantly churning within the theory of plate tectonics.

Glossary

astronomical (ass-truh-NOM-uh-kuhl): extremely large-scale, beyond measurement

cataclysmic (kat-uh-KLIZ-mik): of or having to do with a massive, destructive change

catastrophes (kuh-TASS-truh-feez): a sudden and overwhelming disasters

convection (kuhn-VEC-shuhn): the movement or rise of heat through gasses and/or liquids

convergent (kuhn-VER-juhnt): moving toward another, coming together

divergent (dye-VER-juhnt): moving away or apart from another

dynamic (dye-NAM-ik): changing, in motion toward another form

earthquake (URTH-kwayk): a sudden, violent shaking of the ground

expulsion (ek-SPUHL-shuhn): the forceful outward blast of something out of something else

megathrust (MEG-uh-thruhst): an especially powerful type of earthquake

paleontology (pale-ee-uhn-TOL-uh-jee): the scientific study of fossils and ancient life forms

retrofitting (RET-roh-fit-ing): to add something to a structure after it has already been built

rift (RIFT): a tear, hole, or passageway through a layer of rock in Earth's crust

seismology (size-MOL-uh-jee): the scientific study of earthquakes and movements among the plates making up Earth's crust

stationary (STAY-shuh-nee-ree): not moving, stuck in one place

subduction (sub-DUHK-shuhn): a tectonic process of one plate sliding under another

transform (transs-FORM): a sliding, side-by-side movement of tectonic plates past one another

tsunamis (tsoo-NAH-meez): enormous, destructive waves created by underwater earthquakes or volcanic eruptions

Index

Websites to Visit

www.pubs.usgs.gov/gip/dynamic/dynamic.html

www.iris.edu/hq/programs/education_and_outreach/animations

www.science.nationalgeographic.com/science/earth/inside-the-earth

About the Author

Tom Greve lives in Chicago with his wife Meg, and their two children, Madison and William. He has been contemplating geology and plate tectonics since he was a boy. When he was 11 in May of 1980, he climbed his father's silo to try and see the Mt. St. Helens ash cloud in the western sky.

Meet The Author!
www.meetREMauthors.com